STITCHES

- - - - - - - - - - -

ALSO BY ANNE LAMOTT

Operating Instructions:
A Journal of My Son's First Year

Bird by Bird:
Some Instructions on Writing and Life

Traveling Mercies:
Some Thoughts on Faith

Plan B:
Further Thoughts on Faith

Grace (Eventually):
Thoughts on Faith

Some Assembly Required:
A Journal of My Son's First Son
(with Sam Lamott)

Help, Thanks, Wow:
The Three Essential Prayers

FICTION

Hard Laughter

Rosie

Joe Jones

All New People

Crooked Little Heart

Blue Shoe

Imperfect Birds

STITCHES

A Handbook on Meaning,

Hope and Repair

ANNE LAMOTT

HODDER

First published in Great Britain in 2014 by Hodder & Stoughton
An Hachette UK company

This paperback edition first published in 2016

In association with Riverhead Books
375 Hudson Street, New York 10014
1

The author gratefully acknowledges permission to quote the following:
Jane Kenyon, excerpt from "Briefly It Enters, and Briefly Speaks,"
from Collected Poems. Copyright © 2005 by The Estate of Jane Kenyon.
Reprinted with the permission of The Permissions Company, Inc.,
on behalf of Graywolf Press, www.graywolfpress.org.
Denise Levertov, "In the Japanese tongue . . . ," from Poems 1960–1967.
Copyright © 1966 by Denise Levertov. Reprinted by permission

A CIP catalogue record for this title is available from the British Library

ISBN 978 1 444 78915 7
eBook ISBN 978 1 444 78913 3

Typeset in AndradePro

Printed and bound in the UK by Clays Ltd, St Ives plc

Book design by Amanda Dewey

Hodder & Stoughton policy is to use papers that are natural, renewable
and recyclable products and made from wood grown in sustainable forests.
The logging and manufacturing processes are expected to conform to the
environmental regulations of the country of origin.

Hodder & Stoughton Ltd
Carmelite House
50 Victoria Embankment
London EC4Y 0DZ

www.hodder.co.uk

This is dedicated to
Neshama Franklin.

I don't know Who—or what—put the question, I don't know when it was put. I don't even remember answering. But at some moment I did answer Yes to Someone—or Something—and from that hour I was certain that existence is meaningful and that, therefore, my life, in self-surrender, had a goal.

—Dag Hammarskjöld, *Markings*

STITCHES

- - - - - - - - - - -

One

BEGINNING

It can be too sad here. We so often lose our way. It is easy to sense and embrace meaning when life is on track. When there is a feeling of fullness—having love, goodness, family, work, maybe God as parts of life—it's easier to navigate around the sadness that you inevitably stumble across. Life holds beauty, magic and anguish. Sometimes sorrow is unavoidable, even when your kids are little, when the marvels of your children, and your parental amazement, are all the meaning you need to sustain you, or when you have landed the job and salary for which you've always longed, or the mate. And then the phone rings, the mail comes, or you turn on the TV.

Where do we even begin in the presence of evil or catastrophe—dead or deeply lost children, a young wife's melanoma, polar bears floating out to sea on scraps of ice? What is the point of it all when we experience the vortex of interminable depression or, conversely, when we recognize that time is tearing past us like giddy greyhounds? It's frightening and disorienting that time skates by so fast, and while it's not as bad as being embedded in the quicksand of loss, we're filled with dread each time we notice life hotfoot it out of town.

One rarely knows where to begin the search for meaning, though by necessity, we can only start where we are.

That would be fine, when where we find ourselves turns out to be bearable. What about when it isn't—after 9/11, for instance, or a suicide in the family?

I really don't have a clue.

I do know it somehow has to do with sticking together as we try to make sense of chaos, and that seems a way to begin. We could start with something relatively easy: C. S. Lewis famously said about forgiveness, "If we really want to learn how to forgive, perhaps we had better start with something easier than the Gestapo."

Maybe, counterintuitively, it makes sense to start right off with hard, rather than easy: Where is life's meaning after Katrina, or an unwanted divorce?

If we're pressed for an answer, most of us would say that most of the time we find plenty of significance in life as it unfurls in front of us like a carpet runner—at least when it goes as expected, day by day, with our families and a few close friends. We have our jobs and those we work or play or worship or recover with as we try to feel a deeper sense of immediacy or spirit or playfulness. Most people in the world are striving simply to feed their kids and hang on. We try to help where we can, and try to survive our own trials and stresses, illnesses and elections. We work really hard at not being driven crazy by noise and speed and extremely annoying people, whose names we are too polite to mention. We try not to be tripped up by major global sadness, difficulties in our families or the death of old pets.

People like to say that it—significance, import— is all about the family. But lots of people do not have rich networks of hilarious uncles and adorable cousins, who all live nearby, to help them. Many people have truly awful families: insane, abusive, repressive. So we work hard, we enjoy life as we can, we endure. We try to help ourselves and one another. We try to be more present and less petty. Some days go better than others. We look for solace in nature and art and maybe, if we are lucky, the quiet satisfaction of our homes.

Is solace meaning? I don't know. But it's pretty close.

The kids say, "It is what it is." They can say this with a straight face since they have not had kids yet. I remember my youth, and having that same great confidence in bumper stickers and my own thinking. Say it's true: It is what it is. We're social, tribal, musical animals, walking percussion instruments. Most of us do the best we can. We show up. We strive for gratitude, and try not to be such babies.

And then there's a mass shooting, a nuclear plant melts down, just as a niece is born, or as you find love. The world is coming to an end. I hate that. In environmental ways, it's true, and in existential ways, it has been since the day each of us was born.

It's pretty easy to think you know the meaning of life when your children are small, if they come with all their parts and you get to live in that amazing cocoon of oneness and baby smells. But what if your perfect child becomes sick, obese, an addict or a homeless adult? What if you wake up at sixty and realize that you forgot to wake up, and you never became the person you were born to be, and now your hair is falling out?

You're thinking about this for the first time when maybe it's a little late. Your life is two-thirds over, or you're still relatively young, but your girl went from being two years old to being eleven in what felt like eighteen months, and then in what felt like eight weeks to fifteen, where she has been now, sharply dressed as a bitter young stripper, for as long as you can fricking remember.

Oh, honey, buckle up. It gets worse.

Where is meaning in the meteoric passage of time, the speed in which our lives are spent? Where is meaning in the pits? In the suffering? I think these questions are worth asking.

– – – – – –

Christians would say the answer is simple. Life's meaning is to seek union with God and be Jesus' hands and eyes for the people who need help and companionship. AA might also say it is simple: to stay sober one day at a time and help other alcoholics achieve sobriety. For Buddhists, the answer is mindfulness, kindness and trying to remember to breathe every so often. Environmentalists want to save the planet for all species—or at least a number of them—and so forth.

Ram Dass, who described himself as a Hin-Jew, said that ultimately we're all just walking each other home. I love that. I try to live by it.

These are true and rich philosophies, but often only on good days.

What follows here is intended to be useful on the bad days.

Like life, this book is a patchwork of moments, memories, connections and stories that I've found help steer me in the direction of answers that will hold, for now and even over time. They are observations that in troubled times help me find my way once again to what T. S. Eliot called "the still point of the turning world."

For instance, maybe we can all agree that meaning is always going to have to do with love, and furthermore, that children should not get cancer, or be shot, and that our old must be cared for. Is there really any disagreement on these points? What about when your whole world goes crazy, your body or mind is on the fritz, or your family or government betrays you? What, then, can we agree on? Is anything always true? And if so, why did some of us not get the memo?

This is not a book on Christian meaning, but some of Christianity's language and symbols can be useful: doves of comfort and peace, the prodigal son, lepers, Samaritans, loaves of bread. We all know hopelessness; we know Christ crucified when we see it—in the slums of India and Oakland; passed out on city sidewalks; in someone's early, painful death. We know from resurrection. If I use the word "God," I sure don't mean an old man in the sky who loves the occasional goat sacrifice. I mean "God" as Jane Kenyon described God: "I am food on the prisoner's plate . . . / the patient gardener / of the dry and weedy garden . . . / the stone step, / the latch, and the working hinge." I mean "God" as shorthand for the Good, for the animating energy of love; for Life, for the light that radiates from within people and from above; in the energies of nature, even in our rough, messy selves.

So when hardships and terror appear in our lives, we first ask "Why?" I usually add, "Would it have been so much skin off Your teeth to cut us some slack here?" But then I remember that "Why?" is rarely a useful question. After that, we ask, in a cry from our hearts: What on earth are we supposed to do? It's perfectly rational to expect or hope for an answer from God—I've never thought Job was being unreasonable. I personally would like a lot more stuff around here to make sense. But when something ghastly happens, it is not helpful to many people if you say that it's all part of God's perfect plan, or that it's for the highest good of every person in the drama, or that more will be revealed, even if that is all true. Because at least for me, if someone's cute position minimizes the crucifixion, it's bullshit. Which I say with love.

To use just one Christian example: Christ really did suffer, as the innocent of the earth really do suffer. It's the ongoing tragedy of humans. Our lives and humanity are untidy: disorganized and careworn. Life on earth is often a raunchy and violent experience. It can be agony just to get through the day.

And yet, I do believe there is ultimately meaning in the chaos, and also in the doldrums. What I resist is not the truth but when people put a pretty bow on scary things instead of saying, "This is a nightmare. I hate everything. I'm going to go hide in the garage."

I asked a wise friend, "Is there meaning in what happened in the slaughter at the Sandy Hook school in Newtown?" He said, "Not yet."

Part of this is that we witness such terrible suffering here. Children suffer so; Christ suffers. Then there is the hope of resurrection. Death is not necessarily the enemy, or the end of the story.

I assume that the murdered children in Connecticut were welcomed home at the moment of their deaths. I know in my heart that somehow their families have come through and begun to live again. Yet we have to admit the nightmare and not pretend that it wasn't heinous and agonizing. It wasn't a metaphor; it was the end of the world. Certain spiritual traditions could say about Hiroshima, Oh, it's the whole world passing away. Same with the tsunami in Indonesia.

Well, I don't know.

My understanding of incarnation is that we are not served by getting away from the grubbiness of suffering. Sometimes we feel that we are barely pulling ourselves forward through a tight tunnel on badly scraped-up elbows. But we do come out the other side, exhausted and changed.

It would be great if we could shop, sleep or date our way out of this. Sometimes we think we can, but it feels that way only for a while. To heal, it seems we have to stand in the middle of the horror, at the foot of the cross, and wait out another's suffering where that person can see us. To be honest, that sucks. It's the worst, even if you are the mother of God.

Mary didn't say, "Oh, he'll be back in a couple of days." She didn't know this. She stood with her son in the deep unknowing as he died.

Yet no matter what happens to us—to our children, to our town, to our world—we feel it is still a gift to be human and to have a human life, as long as we ignore the commercials and advertisements and the static that the world beams at us, and understand that we and our children are going to get knocked around, sometimes so cruelly that it will take our breath away. Life can be wild, hard and sweet, but it can also be wild, hard and cruel.

The bad news is that after the suffering, we wait at the empty tomb for a while, the body of our beloved gone, grieving an unsurvivable loss.

It's a terrible system.

But the good news is that then there is new life.

Wildflowers bloom again.

That's it? you ask. That's all you've got?

No. I've also got bulbs. Well. They're both such surprises. Wildflowers stop you in your hiking tracks. You want to savor the colors and scents, let them breathe you in, let yourself be amazed. And bulbs that grow in the cold rocky dirt remind us that no one is lost.

Is that really even true? Wasn't the Newtown shooter lost?

Who knows? There's some disagreement here. I can't believe that a God of love could throw this kid away. It was not his fault that he was so sick.

Whether we like it or not, we are somehow interconnected with the shooter, because we are connected to all of life. Thomas Merton wrote, "The one truth that would help us begin to solve our ethical and political problems [is] that we are *all* more or less wrong, that we are *all* at fault, *all* limited and obstructed by our mixed motives, our self-deception, our greed, our self-righteousness and our tendency to aggression and hypocrisy."

Obviously we are worlds away from the shooter. But somehow he was part of the human family. We breathed the same air he did. Some of us choose to believe we are somehow all from God, huddled on this planet, surrounded by a hundred billion other galaxies, and yet will somehow all return to God.

Walt Whitman wrote, "Nothing is ever really lost, or can be lost, / No birth, identity, form—no object of the world. / Nor life, nor force, nor any visible thing"—although I have to add that evil, sickness, death and there being a hundred billion other galaxies sure complicate the picture. So I could be wrong.

Whether I'm wrong or not, though, most of us have figured out that we have to do what's in front of us and keep doing it. We clean up beaches after oil spills. We rebuild whole towns after hurricanes and tornadoes. We return calls and library books. We get people water. Some of us even pray. Every time we choose the good action or response, the decent, the valuable, it builds, incrementally, to renewal, resurrection, the place of newness, freedom, justice. The equation is: life, death, resurrection, hope. The horror is real, and so you make casseroles for your neighbor, organize an overseas clothing drive, and do your laundry. You can also offer to do other people's laundry, if they have recently had any random babies or surgeries.

We live stitch by stitch, when we're lucky. If you fixate on the big picture, the whole shebang, the overview, you miss the stitching. And maybe the stitching is crude, or it is unraveling, but if it were precise, we'd pretend that life was just fine and running like a Swiss watch. This is not helpful if on the inside our understanding is that life is more often a cuckoo clock with rusty gears.

In the aftermath of loss, we do what we've always done, although we are changed, maybe more afraid. We do what we can, as well as we can. My pastor, Veronica, one Sunday told the story of a sparrow lying in the street with its legs straight up in the air, sweating a little under its feathery arms. A warhorse walks up to the bird and asks, "What on earth are you doing?" The sparrow replies, "I heard the sky was falling, and I wanted to help." The horse laughs a big, loud, sneering horse laugh, and says, "Do you *really* think you're going to hold back the sky, with those scrawny little legs?"

And the sparrow says, "One does what one can."

So what can I do? Not much. Mother Teresa said that none of us can do great things, but we can do small things with great love. This reminder has saved me many times. So I showed up to teach Sunday school two days after the Newtown shootings. I didn't overthink what I would say, because I always end up telling the kids the same things: that they are loved and chosen, that the light shines in the darkness, and the darkness has not overcome it; and to keep trusting God, no matter what things looks like and no matter how long an upswing takes. If something awful has occurred, I ask the kids at Sunday school if they want to talk about what has happened, or if they would rather make art.

One hundred percent of the time, they would rather make art.

We always begin by lighting a candle, although we have switched to an electric light in a votive holder instead of actual wax, because once someone in the class managed to singe the ends of her hair on a real candle.

Then we pray to try to be good and kind to one another. We read a short passage of Scripture, talk about it and try to learn something together about our lives and God's love. And then, as in all great religious traditions, we overeat.

That Sunday after Newtown, I decided we would make angels out of coffee filters. Years ago I located a great website on crafts you can make from coffee filters. We've made a garland of coffee-filter doves for Martin Luther King Jr.'s birthday, and for Easter we make bright coffee-filter butterflies, and chrysalises of paper-towel rolls into which we tuck the butterflies until Easter morning. Nothing looks more dead than a cocoon: hard, immobile, ugly, particularly when it's made out of a cardboard tube from an empty roll of Bounty. And yet, just wait.

I'd intended to bring my stapler from home to make it easier to put the angels together, but I conveniently left it on the kitchen table. At least we had coffee filters and markers at church.

There were only two students that day, both young teenagers who are differently abled. The boy has been living for years with brain cancer, which led to a bleed that has left him with a brain injury. So he talks sort of funny. The other student is a gorgeous girl, who was the person who singed her hair on the candle flame. (You thought it was me, didn't you?) She also talks in an unusual way.

I read them a subversive verse from Luke: "And

it came to pass, that the beggar died, and was carried by the angels into Abraham's bosom." I told them that angels are always around, messengers of God's love, to revive us when we are weary or in an ugly place and to help us cross over when we die. Then I opened a nice fresh package of round white coffee filters.

"Oh, no," the girl said, bending over in her chair so that she smashed her forehead on the table. I asked if she was hurt. No motion or sound. Then, bleating, "Not the coffee filters again."

Mason, on the other hand, beamed.

I sighed and somehow, with my charm and legendary patience, got the girl up and running.

We colored our coffee filters with markers. While we worked, I talked in a general way about what good people can do in the face of great sorrow. We help some time pass for those suffering. We sit with them in their hopeless pain and feel terrible with them, without trying to fix them with platitudes; doing this with them is just about the most gracious gift we have to offer. We give up what we think *we* should be doing, or think *we* need to get done, to keep them company.

We help them to bear being in time and space during unbearable times and spaces.

I would add that, in general, time and space have not been my strong suits.

I would like to be able to explain the world to these loved, lovely and challenged children that would help them understand the meaning of life and make sense of their differentness. This under-standing might have made a big difference in my life fifty years ago. But there can be meaning without having things making sense. Humanity is meaning. It is a synonym for the best of being human—thoughtful, sensitive, caring and com-passionate.

I asked them if they knew what "humane" meant.

The girl raised her hand. "It means, *Why* are all of our projects about coffee filters?"

She always makes me laugh. I gave her a big kiss on the head. I told the kids that humanity meant decency and heart, and that along with love, it was the solution to all problems. The girl sighed and said, "Yeah, yeah, yeah." What a paradox: that we connect with God, with divinity, in our flesh and blood and time and space. We connect with God in our humanity. A great truth, attributed to Emily Dickinson, is that "hope inspires the good to reveal itself." This is almost all I ever need to remember. Gravity and sadness yank us down, and hope gives us a nudge to help one another get back up or to sit with the fallen on the ground, in the abyss, in solidarity.

After we colored our coffee-filter wings, we spritzed them with water, so that the dyes ran slightly. While the filters dried, we had our snacks: string cheese, pears and Capri Sun, the living water of most Sunday schools. We made our angels' heads with a second filter each, scrunched up around balled-up Kleenex, secured with embroidery thread. This gave the angels an unfortunate garroted look, but the heads held, which is all that ever matters. The remaining paper that spread out beneath was the bodies.

At this point, it would have been fabulous if a certain special someone had remembered to bring the stapler from home, because we had to attach the angels to their fabulous tie-dyed and now fairly dry wings. Instead, I got out my tiny travel sewing kit and stitched the wings to the bodies, like the love children of Betsy Ross and Wavy Gravy, and then fluffed out the brightly colored filters for maximum angelic wingspan.

The children loved them, and I knew the parents would, too. The angels were just completely fabulous. Then Mason made an astonishing comment. He said to the girl, adamantly, in his slightly garbled and mumbly way, "You know, I used to have brain cancer. I was in a coma, and then I was *here* again."

I had to close my eyes at the beauty of his understanding—that he was *here* again. He had woken up, as we are all called to do. I said, "You are a miracle."

The girl asked me, in her own slightly garbled way, "Why does he talk so funny?"

Mason didn't seem to notice. He said, "Yes, I am a miracle."

Then he raised his arms and fists like Muscleman.

Two

THE OVERLY SENSITIVE CHILD

Augustine's insight that to search for God is to have found God is deeply profound, because the belief we hold in the existence of another world opens space within us, and around us, which creates a more radiant reality. A radiance is inside us, just as it is visible outside us, and to seek it is maybe to catch a glimpse from time to time of a light within, of a candle at the window of our heart, of a home somewhere inside.

I rarely felt at home as a child, nor did I feel that the earth was my real home. I was a girl who found it scary and confusing to be on this particular planet at all. Like most girls, I always tried to be a good sport about this sense of alienation and basic unworthiness, but it wasn't easy.

My brothers and I were not encouraged to search for God, the obvious source of solace, but we three kids were led to the world of books, which to us was just as good. We found in books the divine plop, the joy of settling down deeply into something, worlds and realities greater than our own troubled minds. All of life, for me, begins with books and art. I was entirely engaged and content when I read *Mr. Popper's Penguins* and *Henry and Beezus* or listened to my father read us *Just So Stories* and *Treasure Island*, or when a teacher helped the class make spooky crayon scratch-boards, or puppets with rags and Popsicle sticks.

When you love something like reading—or drawing or music or nature—it surrounds you with a sense of connection to something great. If you are lucky enough to know this, then your search for meaning involves whatever that Something is. It's an alchemical blend of affinity and focus that takes us to a place within that feels as close as we ever get to "home." It's like pulling into our own train station after a long trip—joy, relief, a pleasant exhaustion.

Barry Lopez wrote, "All that is holding us together [is] stories and compassion." If a writer or artist creates from a place of truth and spirit and generosity, then I may be able to enter and ride this person's train back to my own station. It's the same with beautiful music and art.

Beauty is meaning.

Rarely did anyone encourage my brothers and me to spend our time searching for reality beneath the obvious pleasures of the composition. Our lives buzzed by. The grown-ups we trusted did not share the news that life was going to include deep isolation, or that the culture's fixation on achievement would be spiritually crippling to those of more gentle character. No one mentioned the peace that was possible in surrender to a power greater than oneself, unless it was to an older sibling, when resistance was futile anyway. Teachers forgot to mention that we could be filled only by the truth that suffuses our heart, presence, humanity. So a lot of us raced around the rat exercise wheel, to get good grades and positions, to get into the best colleges and companies, and to keep our weight down.

Most of us have done fairly well in our lives. We learned how to run on that one wheel, but now we want a refund.

Most people in most families aren't going to feel, "Oh, great, Jack has embarked on a search for meaning. And he's writing a family memoir! How great." To the world, Jack has figured out the correct meaning: He's got a mate, a house, a job, children. He's got real stuff that he should fully attend to. At best, seeking his own truth is very nice, but it's beside the point. At worst, one would worry that he was beginning to resemble a native Californian.

It is not now and never was in anybody's best interest for you to be a seeker. It's actually in everybody's worst interest. It's not convenient for the family. It may make them feel superficial and expendable. You may end up looking nutty and unfocused, which does not reflect well on them. And you may also reveal awkward family secrets, like that your parents were insane, or that they probably should have raised Yorkies instead of human children. Your little search for meaning may keep you from going as far at your school or your company as you might otherwise have gone, if you had had a single-minded devotion to getting ahead. Success shows the world what you're made of, and that your parents were right to all but destroy you to foster this excellence.

Robert Heinlein shook up a lot of us in our teens and twenties. Even the title of his most famous book messed with you: *Stranger in a Strange Land.* That phrase from the Old Testament was everything we'd secretly believed about ourselves all along—that because this place was not our home, it was no wonder we felt so different and estranged, as we were all just trying to pass as human. Heinlein's main character could "grok" another person, which meant to deeply, intuitively, in a cellular way, get past the surface, the armor and the biographies, to the soul, to pure awareness.

When we read this, our mouths dropped open—this was revolutionary material. I was so relieved, because I'd known that with one or two special friends and a rare adult, something subterranean and trippy was going on. We were grokking each other, without even trying. And if there was something to be grokked—a vibrational core in us, a consciousness, an essential self, that was not our charm and successes—then didn't it mean there was some kind of capital-T Truth to seek? Obviously, it was not convenient to pursue this, because you had a big test tomorrow on spores, or an interview with the head of marketing. Maybe then just wasn't the right time.

Maybe now is.

For somebody to be on a search means he or she is involved with these subversive topics, reading and comparing notes with allies, asking questions, daydreaming, brooding.

Even though you have homework to do.

So you—I—stuck to the family plan for a long time, because your success made everyone else so happy, even if you made yourself frantic and half dead trying to achieve it. You couldn't win at this game, and you couldn't stop trying. At least it was a home to return to, no matter how erratic, which is better than no home.

If you were raised in the 1950s or 1960s, and grasped how scary the world could be, in Birmingham, Vietnam and the house on the corner where the daddy drank, you were diagnosed as being the overly sensitive child. There were entire books written on the subject of the overly sensitive child. What the term meant was that you noticed how unhappy or crazy your parents were. Also, you worried about global starvation, animals at the pound who didn't get adopted, and smog. What a nut. You looked into things too deeply, and you noticed things that not many others could see, and this exasperated your parents and teachers. They said, "You need to have thicker skin!" That would have been excellent, but you couldn't go buy thicker skin at the five-and-dime.

Any healthy half-awake person is occasionally going to be pierced with a sense of the unfairness and the catastrophe of life for ninety-five percent of the people on this earth. However, if you re-acted, or cried, or raised the subject at all, you were being a worrywart.

I couldn't go to the dog pound to help pick out our family pets, because of the dogs we left behind. I couldn't go to Disney movies, because at the end, the mother of the species was usually taken out to the back and shot. I'd cry. What a stick-in-the-mud. This was the technical term, delivered in a sharp, scolding voice, which further calmed and reassured the child.

As far as I can recall, none of the adults in my life ever once remembered to say, "Some people have a thick skin and you don't. Your heart is really open and that is going to cause pain, but that is an appropriate response to this world. The cost is high, but the blessing of being compassionate is beyond your wildest dreams. However, you're not going to feel that a lot in seventh grade. Just hang on."

I was raised in a family where none of us ever raised a voice, so there was no room to express feelings of rage or even unabashed joy—a little bashed joy, here or there, or being mildly disgruntled. We children were little Marcel Marceaus, tiptoeing about in our invisible boxes. No one ever yelled in a bad marriage that lasted twenty-seven years. My parents went cold and remote. They spoke in clipped phrases of erudite contempt for each other.

If you grew up around alcoholism, one of the first things you learned to do was agree not to see what was really going on. If you screwed up and said out loud that you thought something scary was happening, grown-ups would say, "Oh, for Pete's sake—what an imagination." This is the best way to gaslight children. It keeps them under control, because if the parent is a mess, the children are doomed. It's best for the child to think he or she is the problem. Then there is toxic hope, which is better than no hope at all, that if the child can do better or need less, the parents will be fine.

People used to come to our house and drink, so our home became a kind of Advent calendar, where you'd open a door and there'd be people passed out or the wrong people kissing each other. If we said anything to my parents, they'd say, "Oh, honey, for Christ's sake, we'd all just been drinking"—as if it were an acceptable explanation, like "Oh, honey, we'd all just been putting thorns in our noses."

I grew up thinking that what I witnessed was probably not true, and not all that big a deal—people had just been drinking, for Pete's sake. If it made me feel worried, well—such was the nature of the overly sensitive child.

But then a miracle occurred. The women's movement burst forth when I was fifteen. That was when I began to believe that life might semi-work out after all. The cavalry had arrived. Women were starting to say that you got to tell the truth now, that you had to tell the truth if you were going to heal and have an authentic life. They told us that people like me—i.e., girls—had all been made to feel crazy, neurotic and hypersensitive; they were mad, too, and finally getting mad was going to help save us, because it allowed our truth to escape from jail.

That was great, but I had to learn new skills. One was to no longer pretend not to see what was going on. If a man in my life was behaving badly on some moral level, I made a commitment to myself that I was going to *see* that, instead of helping him feel better about his horrible behavior. I was going to learn to trust that what I saw was really happening. I was smart and sensitive, and like all children who grew up around alcoholism, I learned to pay too much attention. I saw a button pin once that said: "I'm not tense. I'm just very, very alert." It was how I sidestepped the abyss. I had to learn to be present without paying *quite* so much attention to my poor old overamped mind, because this was the source of most of my unhappiness. And it still is.

The second radical choice I made was to notice and then express the fact that I was filled with rage and grief. Who knew? This was very disloyal to my family, for me to no longer play along with the family plan, but all the ways of pretending that I'd been taught were crippling, life-threatening. They had turned me from a delicious dough of flour, yeast, sugar and salt into a desperately self-conscious pretzel. I've never forgotten when my mother and I attended a rare church service on Easter, when I was eleven or so. The Sunday school teacher gave us Bavarian pretzels as a teaching aid and explained that pretzels began as Easter biscuits, representing children with their arms crossed to their shoulders in an old-fashioned way of prayer. But ever since, whenever I've seen them, I've imagined children in straitjackets, like Wednesday Addams with a Rorschach pretzel.

Until I began to deal with my anger and sadness, there had been an invisible Gardol shield between me and life, wild true beautiful hard crazy life. I started to tear the shield down.

I was good at being good at things. I was good at forward thrust, at moving up ladders. You've never heard of forward thrust? It is the most central principle of American life, the necessity to improve your lot and status at any cost, and to stay one step ahead of the abyss that may open suddenly at your heels. Unfortunately, forward thrust turns out not to be helpful in the search for your true place on earth.

But crashing and burning can help a lot. So, too, can just plain running out of gas.

I quit my last real job, as a writer at a magazine, when I was twenty-one. That was the moment when I lost my place of prestige on the fast track, and slowly, millimeter by millimeter, I started to get found, to discover who I had been born to be, instead of the impossibly small package, all tied up tightly in myself, that I had agreed to be.

That was when I began to learn how to do all the things I had been taught *not* to do. I learned over the years to accept more and more of myself. The doctor and theologian Gerald May said self-acceptance is freedom. I learned to waste a lot more time, which is the opposite of the fourth thing you're told after you're born: Don't waste time. (It comes right after Go clean your room.) The fifth rule is Don't waste paper, but in order to become who I was meant to be, I learned I had to waste more paper, to practice messes, false starts and blunders: these are necessary stops on the route of creativity and emotional growth. To make up for all my papery mistakes, I sent money to the Sierra Club. I had to accept that contrary to my parents' terror of looking bad, almost everybody worth his or her salt was a mess and had been an overly sensitive child. Almost everyone had at one time or another been exposed to the world as being flawed, and human. And that it was *good*, for the development of character and empathy, for the growth of the spirit. Periods in the wilderness or desert were not lost time. You might find life, wildflowers, fossils, sources of water.

I wish there were shortcuts to wisdom and self-knowledge: cuter abysses or three-day spa wilderness experiences. Sadly, it doesn't work that way.

I so resent this.

The American way is to not need help, but to help. One of the hardest lessons I had to learn was that I was going to need a *lot* of help, and for a long time. (Even this morning.) What saved me was that I found gentle, loyal and hilarious companions, which is at the heart of meaning: maybe we don't find a lot of answers to life's tougher questions, but if we find a few true friends, that's even better. They help you see who you truly are, which is not always the loveliest possible version of yourself, but then comes the greatest miracle of all—they still love you. They keep you company as perhaps you become less of a whiny baby, if you accept their help.

And that is so much easier said than done.

I also learned that you didn't come onto this earth as a perfectionist or control freak. You weren't born a person of cringe and contraction. You were born as energy, as life, made of the same stuff as stars, blossoms, breezes. You learned contraction to survive, but that was then. You have paid through the nose—paid but good. It is now your turn to reap.

I never used to take my turn. I always gave my turn away. I helped others have a great turn. I must have had a clipboard by the time I was six, because by then I had a whole caseload of people to keep track of. After they had all gotten a turn, then maybe I could go, if there was time and it didn't bother anyone.

Now I take my turn, as a radical act.

Let me tell you a story. (I told this story in a novel years ago, but I want to tell it now as it really happened.) I bought a small, lovely house when my son was ten. The previous owner had kept three huge scary dogs in the family room on the bottom floor. And the dogs had had tiny hygiene issues. So when we moved in, there was the lingering smell of pee downstairs. I felt as much shame about it as if I'd peed on the floor myself.

First I did what all Americans do: I tried to disguise it. I masked it, sprayed it with copious amounts of Nature's Miracle enzymes. But my miracle didn't come: the family room still smelled. I had the rug professionally shampooed. I got a machine that showed you with blue light where the dog urine was, and I bought products that promised to eradicate it. Fixing unhappy situations is my strong suit, so I was game to try.

It didn't work this time.

I hired a handyman to take up the carpet, but the room still stank, plus it now looked like hell, too, because you could see the floor where it was stained with dog pee—as if I didn't have enough self-esteem issues as it was.

So the handyman pulled up the floorboards. But when the flooring came up, things still smelled, and the blue-light pee-pee machine revealed that the joists had urine soaked into them.

Let me repeat that: The joists of the house I had just moved into had urine soaked into them.

We had to strip the bottom floor down to the foundation.

You know what radical, crazy belief drove me to do that? It was the belief I'd been given by people over the years that I was worthy of a house that was beautiful, and that didn't smell; that my son and I deserved a fresh start, a fresh house that was not a cover-up, built on top of secrets and dog pee.

That was fourteen years ago, and I've never been the same. Deeper and deeper exploration over time and revelation down to the foundation have helped me heal my inside home, too. It goes without saying that difficult problems still arise within, but nowadays as I inch toward sixty, I have collected some hard-won skills, a few banged-up tools, needles and enough thread to make meaningful repairs.

Three

STITCHES

While it is hard to fathom who we are and how we are to live when public chaos shatters our routine, the slow-motion pain of each private death and cataclysm we endure is harder. Each slams us off our feet, yet we have agreed to pretend to be fine again at some point, ideally as soon as possible, so as not to seem self-indulgent or embarrass anybody. Then people can get on with their lives.

Sometimes after a disaster or great loss, when we are hanging on for dear life, we struggle to understand how we will ever be able to experience cohesion and safety again. The aspects of life that we treasure and have gathered over time, because they are lovely and go together, are gone. We may feel as if we've been handed ugly patches for our quilt that clash with one another—brown Hawaiian print, say, along with orange Rob Roy tartan and three squares of vomitous sea-foam upholstery.

At this point, a reasonable person can't help thinking how grotesque life is. It can so suck, to use the theological term. It can be healthy to hate what life has given you, and to insist on being a big mess for a while. This takes great courage. But then, at some point, the better of two choices is to get back up on your feet and live again.

There is the tried-and-true method of "Left foot, right foot, left foot, breathe." Or you can become a fundamentalist, perhaps Opus Dei, or Anabaptist. Or you can start to sew around the quilt squares with the same color embroidery thread. This unifies your incompatible patterns, textures and colors. It's grace as an unexpected bond, grace as surprise.

Stitching with the same color thread might mean regular contact with a few trusted friends, the three people you can currently bear who don't make your skin crawl. Daily rituals, especially walks, even forced marches around the neighborhood, and schedules, whether work or meals with non-awful people, can be the knots you hold on to when you've run out of rope. What if you bordered each square with mossy green thread? Maybe the Hawaiian floral will look peaceful next to the sea foam, palm trees growing near the water. And nothing complements orange like dark green, showcasing a crazy plaid burst of sun.

The unifying colors can decrease the sense of shock, mismatch and jostle that you feel. They may give you respite from the worst of the pain so that some time might tiptoe past. They may give you the momentary illusion that you are getting over this devastating loss, which is not a bad thing.

But what if the great secret insider-trading truth is that you don't ever get over the biggest losses in your life? Is that good news, bad news, or both?

The good news is that if you don't seal up your heart with caulking compound, and instead stay permeable, people stay alive inside you, and maybe outside you, too, forever.

This is also the bad news, not because your heart will continue to hurt forever, but because grief is so frowned upon, so hard for even intimate bystanders to witness, that you will think you must be crazy for not getting over it. You think it's best to keep this a secret, even if it cuts you off from certain aspects of life, like, say, the truth of your heart, and all that is real.

The pain does grow less acute, but the insidious palace lie that we will get over crushing losses means that our emotional GPS can never find true north, as it is based on maps that no longer mention the most important places we have been to.

Pretending that things are nicely boxed up and put away robs us of great riches.

When I die, the people to whom I am closest should grieve forever. They should never quite get over me. Otherwise I will seem dead to them, no matter how close I may secretly be.

My friend Pammy died at the age of thirty-seven, leaving behind an eighteen-month-old daughter. Plus she got shingles two months before her death, the height of misery.

No comment.

Well, okay—*shingles*, two months before she died. God Almighty! You have got to be kidding me.

I refuse to pretend that I ever got over her death. I'm still mad that she was ripped off of a rich life at such a young age, that her daughter didn't get to have a mother, and that I can't talk to her on the phone. But after more than a decade had passed, I knew I had reached a sort of achy détente when I tore up her favorite shirt, which had been in my closet since she died.

Pammy often wore a white linen top from Talbots, a blouse of elegance and simplicity, with a scoop neck, perfect long sleeves that stopped short of her wrists, pearl buttons, and tucks below the shoulders so that it draped just right. Two weeks before she died, when the shingles were over, she asked me to try it on. She wanted to see me in it. The shirt was as flattering on me as it had always been on her, and we both wore it during the last days of her life. We shared it, and then one day she said it was mine. She moved into pajamas.

I thought of the shirt as our slutty surplice, because you could undo the top buttons and let cleavage or a camisole show. The tucks softened the clavicle area, the curving-in place beneath our shoulders that is so vulnerable, where I would duck my head when I was young and shy.

It almost looked like a holy garment, and it was one to me. Every time I put it on I felt beautiful, and I felt the softness and lightness of my friend. It made me feel sad, but also braver, because Pammy had been so brave when she got sick. She had always been much braver than I am: for example, I never traveled, partly because I had no money, but also because I was scared to death of flying, hijackers and snakes. (I am only occasionally afraid of snakes on planes, in the overhead bins, although in my defense, I wasn't *ever*, at all, until the movie *Snakes on a Plane* came out.) Pammy was a great traveler and had visited many distant cities, both alone and with her husband. In fact, they had gone to Morocco to take advantage of the last chance for travel they would have for a while before they adopted their daughter. Come to think of it, they were in Marrakech when Pammy discovered the lump in her breast.

"See?" I said, on the way to the first, bad biopsy. "I told you so. Stay home. With me." But metastatic cancer didn't stop Pammy's plans for adoption or travel. She, Jim and their daughter, Rebecca, flew to Maui two months before she died. They were on Kaua'i when the merciless Category 4 hurricane Iniki landed, in 1992. When she got home, emaciated and depleted, I said to her, "I rest my case." She just smiled.

For years after Pammy died, I wore her blouse, with black pants and a silk scarf, when I had to dress up for a meal or a lecture. It lay lightly but held me in just the right places.

Well after the acute pain of losing her had faded, along with the glory of the shirt, I still could not throw it away. The cloth was getting to be almost as thin as tissue. I was nice to myself about this: Of course we do not want to say good-bye. We do not want to sever the few cords that help us feel there is meaning and safety on this earth.

Then tiny tears appeared in the cotton fabric of the shirt. I mended them. Every so often, I put it away in the back of the closet because I didn't know what else to do with it. Then, months later, I would reach in and pull it out again.

I believe in eternal life, and richer realities

than the one we can see. I believe in a reality that stretches and connects us to other realms that are not of this world, but I guess I didn't entirely trust the dreamy ectoplasmic reach. The shirt was the only guaranteed way to stay in touch with Pammy.

Years after her death, I started thinking mean things about myself, and that holding on to her shirt was pure neurotic clinging. That it was ridiculous. Part of me understood that my hold on it had to do with the excruciating mess and weirdness of my family: how only a handful of people in your lifetime help redeem this mess, so that when one of them dies, hope dies. You never fully recover. You can't.

Yet my contact with Pammy remained deep and important. She had helped me raise my son, and before that, she'd helped raise me from the depths of a crazy life, and before that, she had been my bosom buddy since high school, sharing all those joints, beers, rock concerts, the salvation and new beginning in passing back and forth to each other the first issues of *Ms*.

The shirt had been on her body, and her body

was gone. But I could wear it on mine. Something about this worked for me.

I thought that if I got rid of it, and she were floating free, she might just float away and I'd forget even more about her.

We forget so much. All those memories of great meals, travel, landscapes, conversations, insights, theater, and scenes in distant cities, moments you swore you'd remember forever, so many washed away like Etch A Sketch drawings.

It wasn't even that she didn't come visit. People drop by when they can. I had a visitation from her the other morning, which was as real as my sitting here at my desk. She was laughing with some of our friends. You may say it was just that I was half asleep, and I would say, Thank you for sharing.

I took the shirt on a vacation with my Jesuit friend Tom Weston, to Mexico, where I planned to bury it on the beach, beneath the palm trees. One morning I carried it out to the sand, stood watching the surf, then changed my mind. I carried it back inside and put it in my suitcase for the trip home.

The shirt was loaded with memory and with my baby self, whom Pammy had so mothered, and with my broken heart, and with the joy that she was to me, the lightness, the shared history, her sweet intelligence, how she made me laugh. I'd given talks for years about how when it comes to grieving, the culture lies—you really do not get over the biggest losses, you don't pass through grief in any organized way, and it takes years and infinitely more tears than people want to allot you. Yet the gift of grief is incalculable, in giving you back to yourself. And so, putting my money where my mouth was, I listened to that, and on that beach in Mexico I could tell that I was not ready. I decided to wait.

Then too much time passed, and I looked unhinged. I mean, let go already, right? But if something encapsulated all the qualities of someone you loved, someone who helped keep you afloat, and those parts of life that made any enduring sense, how could you let it go?

Unfortunately, all the stitches couldn't hold together what had dissolved. It was finally about trying to fix the unfixable. The shirt was made of fine things that were meant to dissolve. Maybe we are, too. The fabric had a life, like Pammy had a life, and life dissolves even as you cry out, "Don't leave!"

And because all lives are hard and difficult to understand, you acknowledge the slipperiness of those who died—they got out. You hold on to them because it can be so appalling here, until you can't hold on anymore, because you're not holding on to anything after a while. Either they had a Get out of Jail Free card or they became part of the bigger natural order of things. You can't tether them to earth anymore, because the thread has grown too fine. All you can do is say, "I get it: You are somewhere else now. But little flecks of you remain, like mica in rock, which glint and say: It was all true."

Her shirt said: It was true.

- - - - -

A few years after Tom and I went to Mexico, he took me to Southeast Asia. It was mind-blowing: bright, neon, loud. Some of it seemed brilliant and perennially primitive, some of it was racing to catch up to the modern world in flashes of steel and plastic. It was pagodas, temples and ancient tuk-tuk drivers peddling tourists around in carts to Internet cafés.

In Laos, we walked along the muddy brown Mekong River, such a grievous place when I was a teenager, existentially sickening to remember even now. More bombs were dropped on Laos by Americans during the Vietnam War than on all of Europe during World War II, yet dense green bamboo and jungle have grown over most of the scars. The city of Luang Prabang, between two rivers and below mountains, is hazy, hot, eerie, soft, golden. Everywhere we walked, there were scraggly tattered dogs and cats, and banyan trees and tamarinds, houses built on pilings, frangipanis exuding their perfume to attract the moths, French manor houses from colonial times, ornate temples with their gold-leafed Buddhas, mosaic snakes and dragons, hill tribe people alongside ordinary Laotians and monks and hippies. It was antiquity and *Apocalypse Now* all rolled together. Finally we came to the Nam Khan, a soft green ethereal river surrounded by jungle shrubs and palms and tropical flowers, a place out of time.

And on its banks we found a Swedish hotel, a

European hotel run by a Swede. I kid you not. Tom's people are Swedes. I thought it might be a mirage, and we checked in so quickly that I got whiplash.

When I was finally able to leave the hotel's air-conditioning, we reveled in the sleepiness of the village, gorged on noodly food and wandered through the night market.

The following morning, after breakfast, we took a trip on a longboat with skimpy oilcloth awnings to keep the driving downpour off us as we glided past limestone cliffs. The boat leaked, and I imagined drowning while dreaded river snakes attacked. I took a deep breath, though, and realized I was happy in this great beauty. I was brave woman warrior, or at least brave woman traveler.

The next day was my twenty-second sober birthday. Tom, who had been sober for thirty-four years, said, "It's a start." He's so supportive. The hotel owner stopped by our table on the porch at breakfast, and it turned out he was from the same village in Sweden as Tom's mother. Life is much trippier than first imagined.

Late that afternoon, we hung out at an Internet

café. Then Tom mentioned that a friend used to work here until a krait, a venomous snake without any redeeming qualities, slithered past his boot. I made Tom leave with me. It started to rain again. The rain on the Mekong was exquisite, dusky, foggy. The Lao think the foggy mists are ghosts, and I do, too.

I went back to the hotel, and then the strangest thing happened: I went crazy. I'd been fine, maybe a little overwhelmed by the events of the day, until I checked my cell phone for messages. And there were four in the last hour from my son, Sam, who was in the hospital with a fever and a severely bad throat. My first thought was meningitis. I called him in San Francisco but he didn't pick up or call back. I called my brother to go check on him, but he didn't pick up or call back, either. Tom came by, wanting to go to the night market, but I was too upset, what with a mortally ill son.

Tom left, and I was consumed with fear that Sam was in trouble and with the pain of feeling abandoned. I began to cry, abjectly, like a small child. I rarely cry, but I lay on my side and wept as if someone had told me Sam was dead, the way I

cried when my father died, and the way I cry for
every horrible loss: in a state of metallic isolation.

After an hour or so, I pulled Pammy's shirt out
of my suitcase—of course I had brought it with me—
and began to stroke it like a child stroking the satin
trim of a blankie. I felt her appear beside me on the
bed, like mother Mary used to do when I was coming down off speed or cocaine. I felt her physically:
she was there, in my hotel room. I held on to the
sleeve like we were arm in arm again. I grew calm.

I got some cool water from the small refrig-
erator in the room and turned on the TV. I watched
a tennis match for a while. My head moved back
and forth, side to side, and I found some kind of
primitive rhythm, like a girl on a swing. It got me
through the next hour, until Tom returned.

He came into my room bearing a greasy paper
bag. In it were two crepes from the night market,
one chocolate with raspberry jam, and one chocolate with bananas. They were melty, buttery, gooey.
People tell you that you should never eat the street
food in Southeast Asia, but not to have known to
eat those crepes would have argued a wasted life. I
ate them both like there was no tomorrow, which

there really isn't. Robert Burns said it best: "Life is but a day at most."

Tom sat on my bed with me while I ate. We watched tennis together without speaking much. After a while he honked my nose good night and left.

When the tennis match was over, I turned off the TV and slept.

This is what salvation feels like.

In the morning Sam called to say that he had strep, the bill for whose diagnosis was $1,400. I got to be silently mad and self-righteous about his being such a moron to overreact, while at the same time I could be bathed in his voice and pure relief.

I got up at five the next morning, walked to town to watch people feeding rice and leftovers to a line of monks, a daily ritual of giving alms. It's like going to see the Trevi Fountain in Rome: you have to do it, or God would cradle Her head in Her hands and wonder where She had gone wrong with you.

That day I was wearing Pammy's shirt, over a tank top, with shorts and old-lady walking shoes.

I walked around the town looking for a Christian church. I kept walking along, petting cats—my only protection against snakes—while I waited for Tom to wake up.

When I got back to the hotel, Tom was awake and reading his tattered Bible on the porch. I said, "Can we have church right here?" He looked like a Greyhound bus depot prophet. He said, "After we eat. Because we have bodies, too." We had rolls still warm from the oven, melon, starfruit, pineapple and scrambled eggs.

After we had bused our dishes inside, Tom performed the Eucharist with bits of roll and papaya juice shooters; tiny birds as choir, orange cats for nuns. He read, "Through your goodness we have this bread to offer, which earth has given and human hands have made. It will become for us the bread of life." I felt I was being gently reeled in by a fisherman. Earth has given, human hands have made: wow. I had forgotten once again what a phenomenon this life is, beyond all opinion, category or doctrine.

A boatman came up to us and said he would take us for a slow boat ride in one hour; we should meet him at the makeshift slip on the river. We went over to wait when we finished eating. Men were fishing a few yards away. Family longboats piled with supplies and generations of people floated past. It was raining lightly.

Tom was looking at the fishermen when out of the blue I began to unbutton Pammy's shirt. I took it off and held it one more time. It was almost a rag by now.

He turned to see what I was doing. I put my fingers in a hole near the scooped neck, to get purchase, and ripped it lengthwise, as if I was going to use it to make bandages or a tourniquet to stanch someone's bleeding, or rending it as we do fabric before the altar at church on Ash Wednesday, tearing a piece of improvised sackcloth to signify sadness, repentance and a desire to start over.

I tore the shirt into smaller and smaller scraps and dropped each piece into the river.

Tom and I watched the flotilla bob along on the current, until the last wisp of fabric floated away like a petal, surrounded by leaves from the overhanging jungle shrubs, a bit of rag on the river's horizon. We got up and walked, shoulder to shoulder, along the muddy planks to where the young boatman waited.

Four

MOUNT VISION

Alone, we are doomed, but by the same token, we've learned that people are impossible, even the ones we love most—*especially* the ones we love most: they're damaged, prickly and set in their ways. Also, they've gotten old and a little funny, which can be draining. It is most comfortable to be invisible, to observe life from a distance, at one with our own intoxicating superior thoughts. But comfort and isolation are not where the surprises are. They are not where hope is. Hope tends to appear when we see that all sorts of disparate personalities can come together, no matter how different and jarring they may seem at first. Little kids think all colors or patterns of shirt go with all patterns and colors of pants, and it takes us elders a minute to see that they in fact do. Blue madras shorts can look great with a Peter Max print top, in the right hands—say, of someone who has found a visual rhythm, in patterns that play off each other without being chaotic. I've seen this many times. In life the fussy beautician can be beautiful beside the motorcyclist with neck tats, filling boxes with donated food for Thanksgiving dinners, or reading together on the same ratty couch at the library. Only together do we somehow keep coming through unsurvivable loss, the stress of never knowing how things will shake down, to the biggest miracle of all, that against all odds, we come through the end of the world, again and again—changed but intact (more or less). Emerson wrote, "People wish to be settled; only as far as they are unsettled is there any hope for them." I hate this idea more than I can capture in words, but insofar as I have any idea of "the truth," I believe this to be as true as gravity and grace.

Fifteen years ago, there was a local tragedy. It

was not a mass shooting or a tsunami, but it was devastating still, with four teenage boys at fault.

There is a coastal town of about 1,500 people twenty miles away from where I live, where one of my first memories took place, of splashing with my parents and older brother in warm water that had pooled and warmed after the tide had receded. We used to go to the town fairly often for seafood dinners. It was artsy, hidden away, with gulls and pelicans overhead. We would have picnics there with friends and lots of wine, and elderberry hunts in the fall. On the drive into town, you could pull over, get out of the car and jump into the bay. There are sheltered beaches, tiled in shells and beach glass; and boats and fishermen, shaded lanes and towering trees; and a few overpriced places to eat ("Would you like a croissant? . . . That will be one hundred dollars"). Many of the townspeople go back generations; others came in the sixties. There are a lot of drugs. The colors there—of the water, the rushes, the impossibly rich vegetation—drive people to ecstasy and madness. The palette is Gauguin, wild, the colors of lust.

In 1995, there was a huge and devastating fire on the long, majestic ridge that runs for miles out to the bay. Four older teenage boys from the town had camped at Mount Vision overnight, illegally, had built a campfire, buried it under dirt when they left in the morning, and caused a fire that destroyed 12,000 acres of wilderness area and nearly fifty homes.

Helicopters saved the town with water from the bay; the water was dropped on the pine forest between the town and the burning ridge. But the loss of wildlife was unimaginable: birds, deer, coyote, bobcats, mountain lions, beavers. It was as if a bomb had fallen.

Columnist Jon Carroll at the *San Francisco Chronicle* published a letter from a reader a few weeks after the fire. The writer described the heroism of the firefighters, the community's round-the-clock efforts to save whatever could be saved, the generosity and compassion we've come to expect after natural and man-made catastrophes, the coming together.

The four teenage boys who had accidentally

started the fire turned themselves in early on, with their parents beside them.

How do you jiggle a miracle out of rage, ghastliness, terror, ash, grief and teenage boys?

A firefighter had written a letter to a local paper, which the *Chronicle* letter-writer described, about how carefully the boys had tried to put out the fire. Though they had extinguished the flames, embers were still burning underground. The boys hadn't known this could be a fire danger. They'd left.

After that, even as townspeople continued to share their loss and pain, they also told stories of their worst teenage mistakes and transgressions.

We rarely think our way out of these tight, dark places. Sometimes as a community, though, we take an action together, and somehow something gives. I love the pun in that.

There is one action all grateful and grieving communities take: holding a picnic where speeches are given, tears shed, sighs heaved, everyone overeats, and all that sneaky extra breath helps people start to breathe deeply again. A picnic was held to honor the firefighters. The whole town turned out.

The president of the board of firefighters gave a speech, but at the end, he digressed from what you might have expected him to say.

He talked about how in ancient times, people who did damage to a town were sent to live outside its walls, beyond the pale, or boundary, beyond community, beyond inclusion and protection. He mentioned the four young men who had started the Mount Vision fire, and that he had heard that their families were thinking of moving away. He thought the town should make it clear to the families that they should stay, that they were wanted, that they were needed.

There was sustained applause. People whose houses had burned down came up to the speaker to say they agreed with this plan. The town wanted these young men inside the pale, inside the ring of protection. The author of the letter to the *Chronicle* wrote: "So what seems to me to be happening is that this community, which has just fought so stubbornly to save itself from a holocaust, has turned, almost without missing a beat, to try to save the future of four young men."

If there is a God, and most days I do think there

is, He or She does not need us to bring hope and new life back into our lives, but keeps letting us help.

My young preacher friend Anni pointed out to me that God could do anything God wanted, heal and create through weather or visions or the ever popular tongues of fire, but instead chooses us to be the way, to help, to share, to draw close. To me, that is a terrible idea. No offense. Look at us. Look at the dry bones of the ruined people in Ezekiel. This prophet, who probably looked like a complete nut, had a vision of these bones coming back to life, becoming people again. His compassion and witness were the breeze that stirred them, the spirit, which is an infusion of energy, which is life. He roused them and got them back to their feet. Again, if there is a God, He or She does not need Ezekiel, or the people of this small burnt town, but instead chooses people. What a crazy system.

- - - - - -

A few years later, in a town twenty miles east of Mount Vision, a woman I know had a different kind of catastrophe.

I knew Helen through a mutual friend and assumed she had an ideal life, because she had what we all wanted to have: good looks, smarts, a warm personality, a beloved spouse with whom to grow old. They were comfortable enough, spry, with grown kids and Kodak grandchildren. I used to see this couple on walks, and I envied their marriage, one unit, the community of two, a bulwark against Them—others—the best way to hunker down on walks or in bed or at dinner parties and be protected.

He was charming and amiable. But as she confided one day to our mutual friend, her husband's mind was dissolving.

The ground started to buckle under her, as it does when your beloved's mind is going. You don't know where to put your foot down. You might put it in a hole and break your ankle. Over the months, Helen moved from being companion and spouse to helpmate to nursing aide and interpreter.

Forty years of love, fun and hard times, and yet the best their community and doctors could do was patch together something rough. Two pieces of cloth, forty years before, had become one, fused, and now, like a strip of old cloth, it was attenuated and unraveling.

When you can step back at moments like these and see what is happening, when you watch people you love under fire or evaporating, you realize that the secret of life is patch patch patch. Thread your needle, make a knot, find one place on the other piece of torn cloth where you can make one stitch that will hold. And do it again. And again. And again.

Eventually Helen had to put her husband in a nearby convalescent home. In the beginning, when they were together, they could admire the pieces of their lives, affirm them, and most important, re-member together. When both cloths were together, the threads knew each other.

On bad days, he would cry and plead for her to bring him home. He grew worse, and all they could do was huddle together as his mind and his time ran out.

Everyone in the family was heartbroken. The fabric of the relationship became smaller and smaller, and the marriage was no longer a blanket for the whole family.

A lot of us were there for Helen, by phone and for walks. We could listen, nod, sigh, and not descend into the trough she'd been in. We persuaded her to let others inside; we promised that this was the way up and out of the pit. People showed up, neighbors, relatives, college friends from fifty years before, who came from all over the country.

How can you promise someone that this net will catch her and hold? You can't, really. But it did. After a time there was flow again, and in flow there was connection, so she was not alone. Flow and connection sort of says it all.

Helen and her husband had slivers of courtship for a while, hands touching hands, hands touching arms. She was his salvation, although sometimes he couldn't place her. She went every day to see him. Small moments were what lifted her. From the window at the home, she and her husband saw birds, a deer stepping across the yard, gophers, visions that could fill them for a fleeting second—which is what our lives are made of.

We assume that vision is either the narrow focus or the big sweep, but it actually shifts and is both. Helen's heart was broken, of course, when her husband died.

It was, as Zora Neale Hurston wrote, "the meanest moment of eternity." Yet somehow or other, time passed after his death. Helen's heart had softened, and she had grown strong. She will always be lonely here without her husband, but she loves much of her life again. That's proof enough for me that love is sovereign, that most of the time, love bats last.

And this is what she had to offer when our dear mutual friend's son grew deathly ill: a promise that we do endure, and that out of the wreckage something surprising will rise. Helen was proof that in the cold wind, if you can lean against others, none of you will blow away. You keep each other from falling or help each other get back up. Someone holds out a hand, or even scared old you may hold out a hand, and a person in need reaches for it and hangs on.

We held out our hands to our friend, who lives in another coastal community twenty miles from Helen, twenty miles south of Mount Vision.

ANNE LAMOTT

This friend's grown son, David, more or less lived on the streets for thirty years. He had a small place he could call his own, but he chose to live outdoors. I'd known him since he was a child. He looked like Puck, and he still had an innocence in his face, even surrounded by matted hair. I drove him to his grandmother's funeral in Oakland a few years ago, with his grocery bags of broken electronics, and he bragged about how well he could dine from dumpsters. He was strong from walking all day. He was sweet, smart, aggravating, courtly, alcoholic and mentally ill.

Over the years, his mother welcomed him home once a week or so, when he had not been drinking, for coffee, or soup, or whatever happened to be on the stove. Sometimes love does not look like what you had in mind.

Like most of us, David's mother has tried to be an individual who doesn't ask for help, except for those times when she has been sufficiently injured by life's shrapnel and potholes to be forced to. Another way to put it: She is not a big hugger.

The townspeople had always been friendly to

- 66 -

David, and friendliness is a great blessing when ordinary life for someone is extraordinarily weird.

People always asked his mother about him out of social convention: How is David doing? How are you? Her answer might be, "Oh, about the same," or "Nightmarishly. And yourself?"

Then David had a massive seizure at his cabin, and then another. He was found, half dead, by a friend and brought to an ICU about an hour away. He hung on to life. I hoped he would slip away.

I know God enjoys hearing my take on how best we should all proceed, as I'm always full of useful advice. I'm sure God says either, "Oh, I so love Annie's selfless and evolved thoughts," or else "Jeez. What a head case."

Eventually David was moved out of the ICU into the general hospital population. This was when my friend sank into the pit, when the adrenaline stopped. Where could he go next? I told her, "See him in his wholeness." She told me later that this is what helped her most. When we try to see a damaged person as one of God's regular old customers, instead of a lost cause, it takes the pressure off everybody. We can then loosen our death grip on the person, which usually results in progress for everyone, also known in certain circles as grace.

David learned how to walk again and talk again, only sometimes in gibberish. Whenever I went to visit him at the hospital, he told me how glad he was to meet me; any friend of his mother's and all that.

The people in the town asked after him constantly, and at first my friend dreaded giving them the bad news, that he would probably always have to be institutionalized. But people said, "It must be really hard." They cried for him, they went to visit him. His mother felt like an apprentice or novice at taking in community concern. But answering questions and accepting people's love and agreeing to convey it to him transformed the square of ground on which she stood into a wider swath. It became a dirt road of caring. People said, "Just say the word, and I'm here." And then they were: for rides, errands, good ideas, unforeseen needs, some urgent.

Helen was there, too. She had come through devastation to a new life that she might not love as much as the old one, but (a) who asked? and (b) it could still be a good life that might start to grow on a person, down the road.

Slowly, my old friend began to see her son as tarnished, tweaked, yet also poignant. She had not had any idea how loved David was. She had thought she had a bead on his small, dubious life. But the people in her town had different perspectives.

They told her, "He always came and fixed things for me."

They said, "He was always courtly to me, like a man from another era."

They said, "I loved seeing him on his daily walks, those sturdy brown legs, his pleasure in being outdoors."

She started to learn after all these years who her child was, a strange and friendly man to many people. The more that townspeople shared their details with her, the better she could see him reflected in their faces, in the great insect eye of the town that saw her son from so many directions. He went from being her loved but ruined child, a loner, to also a childhood comrade remembered from the past, a friend to an old lady, a naturalist and someone who helped people repair their electronics, usually for free.

My friend tried to find a good place for David to live when he was well enough to leave the hospital. After a rocky trajectory she put him in a home mainly for aged people with Alzheimer's. He was given strong meds to prevent seizures, escapes and outbursts.

Once again, she dreaded people's questions. What was she going to say? "I put him in the bin. However, it's a *nice* bin." But these people cared. They didn't say, "How can you consign him to a life of locked doors?" What they said was, "We miss him. We care about him, and you."

Because they were there, she felt part of something bigger than her own private suffering. Because she could look at Helen and see that she had survived, and that her husband had had good care until the end, she felt that maybe things might work out for David, too.

And they did. My friend drives to see her son at the home in San Francisco every two weeks. They go for short walks, and they talk about whatever comes up. Sometimes he makes very little sense. It's a beautiful drive, beside and under endless tall trees, past pastures, cows, horses, ponds, farms. Flickering screens of color rush by, dappled patches of road, then such brightness that even dark glasses can't help.

– – – – – –

These two women's lives were sometimes too hard and scary for words; that life can be that way is an unfortunate detail someone forgot to tell you. Their lives had come apart into pieces in a way they'd never agreed to. But out of the pieces they each sewed something together. The parts were rough and homely, because that is the nature of dementia. That is why I've always loved funky rustic quilts more than elegant and maybe lovelier ones. You see the beauty of homeliness and rough patches in how they defy expectations of order and comfort. They have at the same time enormous solemnity and exuberance. They may be made of rags, torn clothes that don't at all go together, but they somehow can be muscular and pretty. The

ANNE LAMOTT

colors are often strong, with a lot of rhythm and
discipline and a crazy sense of order. They're improvised, like jazz, where one thing leads to another, without any idea of exactly where the route
will lead, except that it will refer to something
else maybe already established, or about to be.
Embedded in quilts and jazz are clues to escape
and strength, sanctuary and warmth. The world is
always going to be dangerous, and people get
badly banged up, but how can there be more meaning than helping one another stand up in a wind
and stay warm?

Five

REMNANTS

M any people did help me to stand up in July 1986 when I stopped drinking.

For the first thirty-two years of my life, I sought insight and meaning from men and women much like the people in my family—which is to say, they were overeducated and fun to be with, and they drank. Then I got sober, and a few years later had a child—the two most extreme decisions of my life.

Afterward, it turned out that some of the sober people who mentored me through sobriety's monkey mazes had not been housebroken for long or practicing good dental hygiene. They taught me that I would often not get my way, which was good for me but would feel terrible, and that life was erratic, beautiful and impossible. They taught me that maturity was the ability to live with unresolved problems. They taught me that truth was not going to fit on a bumper sticker, much as I would have liked. They taught me—or tried to teach me—humility. This was not my strong suit. Humiliation? Check. Egomania? Check. With their help I learned that raising children is hard, that people are ruined, and that friends die, and that still I didn't need to pick up a drink. The best people could become completely unhinged or act like total asshats. And no matter how great we looked, everything would pass away, especially the stuff we loved the most and could not live without.

They also taught me that God or life or something had set up a system of emergency tents among us, like *M*A*S*H* tents, and would help us work together, and help us work through our more repellent shortcomings, although this, unfortunately, would happen only over time.

They taught me that being of service, an ally to the lonely and suffering, a big-girl helper to underdogs, was my best shot at happiness. They taught me that most of my good ideas were not helpful, and that all of my ideas after ten p.m. were especially unhelpful. They taught me to pay attention, but not so much attention to my tiny princess mind.

So I pay attention to almost every Oregon junco I see on my hikes, these most ordinary tiny gray birds, the males with black heads. They weigh only an ounce, even with all those bones and feathers, all those birdy insides, feet and beaks. They hop around on the ground, near trees, in forests, on lawns. When I watch and listen, they make me laugh, and this fills me with hope.

I have always given everyone in the world lots of help and hope and my own supplies of life force, but the sober people taught me it was okay to *ask* for help, even a lot of help. This was stunning. And it turned out that there was always someone around who could help me with almost everything that came up, and that some people seem to have been assigned to me, as I had been assigned to other people.

These people, like God, have skills and know

things. One friend is a brilliant editor. One friend can fix anything that breaks down in my house. One friend makes exquisite purses.

One friend, my spiritual mentor and indefatigable advocate Bonnie, has answered every tough parenting and spiritual question I've asked her. Her words, like goldenseal, have helped heal my mind to the extent that I no longer have to refer to her very often as Horrible Bonnie, just because she loves me so much.

My friend Neshama sews. She is a skilled seamstress, in an eccentric sort of tribal-arts way, native funk and flash rather than McCall's patterns, although she made the creamy-white beaded gown for her daughter's wedding from one of those. She repairs and restores all of our stuff, her family's and mine. She altered my baby's clothes, and she fixes my baby's baby clothes now.

She has let out more pairs of my pants than I care to remember or will admit to.

I had four sheer white floor-length curtains from India—via Cost Plus—for the tall, wide windows in the front room of my house. They were lovely. The top halves were designed with heavily appliquéd ovals, filled with white stained-glass foliage. The bottom half was simple, just sheer, calm cotton. My windows look out onto the street, so without curtains, I am exposed to passersby. The curtains are both pretty and as utilitarian as underpants.

I say "had" because I also have a large, moronic black-and-white mutt named Bodhi, who ruined the bottom half of one curtain within months by shredding it with his tusklike toenails, while trying to protect us from the invading postman and the dreaded Oregon juncos. When he was done, the curtain looked like a grass skirt.

I went back to Cost Plus, but the curtains were out of stock, and the store was not getting more till next season, if at all, and they were sold out online.

I took the shredded curtain down but couldn't bring myself to throw it away. The top, appliquéd part was still pristine. Life had not gotten its mitts on this one. This is the only way to keep these things nice and unsoiled—fly them up high where fewer tusks can get to them. Better yet, don't use them at all, and definitely don't have pets.

I took a curtain from the side window and filled in the gap.

About a year later, an assassin, or possibly a junco, breached the front gate, and Bodhi managed to plunge through a formerly tiny tear in the replacement curtain and got stuck in the now enormous hole so that he looked like one of the hippos in tutus in *Fantasia*.

He was very sorry, but these things happen.

I left the curtain with its Bodhi-sized hole up for a while, as a sight gag. I happened to mention to Neshama that there were now two top halves of appliquéd cotton, and no bottoms. She wondered if the two tops could be mated, and ended up taking them home to see what she could do.

This is all that restoration requires most of the time, that one person not give up. For instance, when I was in school, there were a few teachers along the way who must have seen in me a hummingbird of charming achievement, all eyes, bird bones, frizzly hair and a desperation to please and impress. They knew that there was power and beauty deep inside me, but that I was afraid of this and I was in fragments. Men and women alike, old and new at teaching, were like aunties or grandparents in their firm patience with me, in their conviction of my worth. They had a divine curiosity about me—"Hey, who's in there? Are you willing to talk straight and find who you actually are, if I keep you company? Do you want to make friends with your heart? Here—start with this poem."

This is who I want to be in the world. This is who I think we are supposed to be, people who help call forth human beings from deep inside hopelessness.

A month later, Neshama brought back the homely and extraordinary curtain she had fashioned from the two top halves, along with this story:

She had begun the way one does most challenges and works of art, by laying things out, studying them, mulling over possible fixes, rolling back her sleeves, trying things out.

She pinned the two intact appliquéd tops together the best she could, as there were varying layers of appliqué. It took forever. She would measure, pin, groan, give up, try again. Finally she sewed the first primordial horizontal seam, on her old sewing machine.

There was an inch-wide gap in length, so she filled it with a bandwidth of cloth. Then it turned out that the curtains were slightly flared, so she needed to make two long patches for the sides. In a few places there were lumps where too many seams met up. The major seam between the top and bottom contained patches and lumps of appliqué.

She said that a great seamstress would have been able to avoid all these problems with precision measurements. But because she relies on trust and instinct, she worked around all the eccentric problems with bits of odd patchwork funk.

Sewing is a finger-and-heart equivalent of putting one foot in front of the other. If you come from a relatively healthy and loving family, you can make a mistake, go back, take it out or patch it. But there is no one fitting that description around here. I had to be taught that it was even okay to *make* mistakes at the age of thirty-two, by the people who fished me out of the sludge of alcohol, confusion and perfectionism.

These people who did not have perfect records of good dental hygiene knew that the same strength that held me down, like the Lilliputians tying up Gulliver, was the energy that would help me get my life back, help me get *me* back. When that life force was going downward, like an elevator heading for the basement, it was about resisting life, staying numb, shutting out the vague lifelong shame, with old patterns that saved me from hurting worse than I had hurt. The people helped me find meaning and a messy redemption in all the dark nights I had come through, all the brokenness. It was not pretty or impressive, but rather surprising.

As Neshama pressed on with the curtain, she gave me periodic updates on how she was doing: I could tell it was going to be an original life-on-life's-terms creation. If I was going to use this curtain, I simply had to accept that there was no way to fuse the remnants, one with the other, without the seamy lines of overlap and hodgepodge showing.

She stitched a lot by hand, as the thickest lumpy sections did not quite fit under her sewing machine's presser foot. She took small sections, pinned them, stitched them together, undid it, patched, pinned, stitched. Then she did this over and over, again and again.

Here's the true secret of life: We mostly do everything over and over. In the morning, we let the dogs out, make coffee, read the paper, help whoever is around get ready for the day. We do our work. In the afternoon, if we have left, we come home, put down our keys and satchels, let the dogs out, take off constrictive clothing, make a drink or put water on for tea, toast the leftover bit of scone. I love ritual and repetition. Without them, I would be a balloon with a slow leak.

The newly sewn curtain was fabulous, and crazy. Whereas before it had been logical and tranquil, with a lot of fabric art above, dropping to the quiet bottom half, now it was one wild lake of designs. Once it was two torn-up curtains, and now it was a whole, although a whole with issues. It was all oval white stained-glass appliqué with a lumpy tummy. The seams were straight, with overlaps and shadows. It looked like a tumbling trick instead of a delicate Madonna in repose, a Cirque du Soleil finale instead of the *Pietà*. I love it.

Beauty is a miracle of things going together

imperfectly. Now when I look at the curtain, many times a day, I always remember that a large berserk dog had been trapped in the once gauzy bottom. I know there's solace in making do with what you've got, making things a little bit better. What might have been thrown out went from tattered scraps to something majestic and goofy and honest that holds together, that keeps people's eyes off me and my family, yet lets in the light and sun, like a poem or a song.

You have to keep taking the next necessary stitch, and the next one, and the next.

Without stitches, you just have rags.

And we are not rags.

Six

FORWARD

The search is the meaning, the search for beauty, love, kindness and restoration in this difficult, wired and often alien modern world. The miracle is that we are here, that no matter how undone we've been the night before, we wake up every morning and are *still* here. It is phenomenal just to be.

This idea overwhelms some people. I have found that the wonder of life is often most easily recognizable through habits and routines. For instance, if you do your morning in sequence—let out the dogs, get the paper, put water on, feed the cat, have breakfast, get to work—then at some point it is late enough for dessert. Ice cream, June peaches, Brie, Toblerone or a Sauternes. (I would join you in the Sauternes if I did not have to get married or jailed afterward.)

Order and discipline are important to meaning for me. Discipline, I have learned, leads to freedom, and there is meaning in freedom. If you don't do ritual things in order, the paper doesn't read as well, and you'll be thrown off the whole day. But when you can sit for a while at your table, reach for your coffee, look out the window at the sky or some branches, then back down at the paper or a book, everything feels right for the moment, which is maybe all we have.

Seeking and searching for fame won't yield much. We won't be remembered, and that turns out to be good news. Who reads the great Stanley Elkin one generation after his death? Or May Sarton? Or Dawn Powell? Who was Truman's vice president? (Alben W. Barkley.) Becoming famous is of momentary reward, and then stressfully unimportant, like winning the set of steak knives in *Glengarry Glen Ross*.

So there's attention, creation, love and dessert.

Love is the question: How can it possibly be enough this time, in the face of such tragedy, loss or evil? And it is the answer: It will be. How can this family or town make a comeback? The next right action, the breath of time passing, love. Go figure.

- - - - - -

The search for meaning will fill you with a sense of meaning. Otherwise life passes by in about seven weeks, and if you are not paying attention and savoring it as it unfurls, you will wake up one day in deep regret. It's much better to wake up now in deep regret, desperate not to waste more of your life obsessing and striving for meaningless crap. Because you will have finally awakened.

There is meaning in focus, concentration, attention. I now notice almost every single bird that flies by, as well as every single butterfly. I pay attention to most plain old butterflies, not just the ones in tiaras or argyle socks. Butterflies and birds are like one perfect teaspoon of creation.

Tomorrow I am going to make coffee-filter butterflies with my Sunday school kids, with paper-towel-tube chrysalises. I know the same girl will be bitter that all of our projects involve coffee filters. I will read her a beautiful passage of Scripture about wings that she will not appreciate much, and I will give her a waxed-paper bag of the season's first cherries, which she will.

I will ask my kids to consider the beauty of the world, and then I will ask them to think about being stuck and seemingly doomed and in the dark, like a chrysalis. I won't rant about the tragedy of global warming or the decimation of the butterfly populations and the apocalyptic implications of that, or how when these kids reach college there will be only a few thousand panting, very tense butterflies arriving in our county over the winter. I know that these kids, like all decent humans, will spend some of their lives swimming in sadness. But I want them to keep going to Muir Woods or the beach at Tennessee Valley during the monarch migrations. I want them to cling to hope, no matter the cost. So I'll get them excited about the process of caterpillar, chrysalis, butterfly. Wow. Amazing. Then we'll go outside and find a few butterflies and chase after them.

- - - - - -

My fantastic friend Barbara died recently of ALS, better known as Lou Gehrig's disease. She was not afraid, or if she was, I didn't see it much, because she was still in love with her partner of nearly forty years, still got outside every day, had an adoring community of friends and a tenderhearted rabbi with worldly exposure and a broad emotional vocabulary who came by often to study the Torah with her.

Barbara started out as a lawyer, but after beating breast cancer twenty years ago, she made her life about teaching women the truth about breast cancer: how to beat it, how to live with it, how to walk other people through it, how to avoid makeup and household products with carcinogens, and how to fight the corporations that make a profit from it. (At her funeral, she was eulogized as having died after a long and courageous battle with the breast cancer industry.) Then she got ALS. It completely sucked.

Yet I saw more meaning in Barbara's last two years and slow death than I have seen in many highly successful ongoing lives. People sometimes say that without death, life would have no meaning. But death was never the meaning of their lives, even though they had to say good-bye to so many friends with breast cancer. Love was, and getting nourishment, however they could. Barbara had a feeding tube for the last four months or so, but she smiled and laughed as much as ever. Laughter is deliverance, bubbly salvation. She lived to see her partner, Susie, a little longer, and then a little longer. They read, saw friends, immersed themselves in nature. They watched the Giants win the World Series twice in three years, which, believe this old San Franciscan, made a mockery of death.

I asked Barbara one day at the end of her life how she was. She had lost the use of her voice by then, so she typed into her computer translation device, "I am." Then she typed some more and the computer voice said, "The disease progresses." Yes. I could see this with my own eyes.

Then she wrote, "The beat goes on." Those four words continue to ring through the chambers of my mind.

When we agree to (or get tricked into) being part of something bigger than our own wired, fixated minds, we are saved. When we search for something larger than our own selves to hook into, we can come through whatever life throws at us.

"Larger" can mean a great cause, a project of restoration, or it can mean a heightened, expansive sense of the now. Here is just one sentence by Denise Levertov: "In the Japanese tongue of the mind's eye one two syllable word tells of the fringe of rain clinging to the eaves and of the grey-green fronds of wild parsley." Larger can mean a six-pound addition to the family—nothing is larger than a newborn—and it can mean mountains, fjords and sand dunes.

The Great Sculptor has made dunes all over the world with drifts of sand that stretch for miles without flaws, all heart-soaring curves and drops, mountain ranges in miniature.

Under the moonlight, you can make your shadow enormous. You feel both tiny and big. You can stagger around making huge shadows as you charge down the dunes. You can make yourself as small as a doll and almost disappear, and then, in an instant, as big as a Cyclops. It's like you brought a whole cast of scary troll characters with you out into the moonlight, which you can bring forth at your pleasure, all these aspects of who you were inside all along.

We, too, are shadow and light. We are not supposed to know this, or be all these different facets of humanity, bright and dark. We are raised to be bright and shiny, but there is meaning in the acceptance of our dusky and dappled side, and also in defiance.

— — — — —

There is so much meaning in stories told around a campfire, or in bed, or at the movies. People who teach others to read or to navigate a library, who don't give up on slow or challenged students, will get the best seats in heaven. I don't know a lot, but I know this to be true.

My brother teaches special education at a local high school. I think he will be seated near the

Godiva chocolate fountain on the other side of eternity. Our father taught English and writing to the prisoners at San Quentin in the fifties and sixties. All good teachers know that inside a remote or angry person is a soul, way deep down, capable of a full human life—a person with hope of a better story, who has allies, and can read.

My father and brother had to find a resource deep down inside themselves, too, because hope is a conversation. They had to be able to tap into something more authentic than the Lamott default skills of being on, of charm, and our standard offer of affection: I love you, here are the rules.

To me, teaching is a holy calling, especially with students less likely to succeed. It's the gift not only of not giving up on people, but of even figuring out where to begin.

You start wherever you can. You see a great need, so you thread a needle, you tie a knot in your thread. You find one place in the cloth through which to take one stitch, one simple stitch, nothing fancy, just one that's strong and true. The knot will anchor your thread. Once that's done, you take one more stitch—teach someone the alphabet, say, no matter how long that takes, and then how to read Dr. Seuss, and *Charlotte's Web*, and *A Wrinkle in Time*, and then, while you're at it, how to get a GED. Empathy is meaning.

Finally, darning: Most good families in the 1950s had wooden darning eggs. You may not have ever seen one, and no, there isn't an app for it, but it is an egg-shaped piece of wood, stone or ceramic, that fits inside most socks. (Some reform families used darning eggs with handles, but not us. We were purists.) You may not have heard the word "darning" in years. So many people nowadays haven't learned how to sew at all, but back then, most women and girls were taught how to sew, and all of the fathers I knew had served in World War II or Korea and knew how to make basic repairs, and even darn.

Darning is to send parallel threads through the damage in socks and sweaters, in and out, in and out, back and forth, over and under, and somehow, you have a piece of fabric again—such as the heel of a sock, that's good enough again, against all odds. This is sort of a miracle—good enough again.

Wow. You're weaving, in effect, starting with rag-
gedy edges, going back a bit to the one spot that can
still hold new thread.

It definitely helps to have a darning egg as you
go through life. Trust me on this.

I have found that my tiny church, St. Andrew
Presbyterian, has given me a shape to work
against—a darning egg—for the last thirty years,
what with all these holes. We have a choir of eight
people who open their mouths, and a huge sound
comes out, a mix of joy, pain, faith and conversa-
tional exposition. Spirit rises and falls in the voices,
the choir's and ours.

The singing is full-throated and clear, like the
sound your finger makes when you run it around
the rim of a crystal glass. It is like African singing
where people call from various spots and create
one sound. Twenty minutes after the first cave
children started kicking around the first improvised balls, people started singing. Half an hour
later, they found harmonies.

Even with a couple of exceptional singers in
the choir, you hear a solid spirit of song, rather

than how individuals personally embellish it. The rising and falling is like all of us leaning forward together, then leaning backward on our heels, then coming forward together again. Spirit flows, and the sounds keep stirring that spirit, as the breezes from the high open windows above us keep stirring the air.

Sometimes the pianist hits a few false notes, or the soloist warbles, and some of us sing along enthusiastically in the wrong key and the old people's voices dim. But we all keep singing, a mix of magnificence and plainsong that is beautiful, and the hymn plays on.

Acknowledgments

Thank you to everyone at Riverhead Books, especially my editor Jake Morrissey, publisher Geoff Kloske, copy editor Anna Jardine, and the amazing rascally rabbits in the publicity, marketing and editorial departments—Katie Freeman, Lydia Hirt, Alexandra Cardia.

Love and much gratitude to my agent, Sarah Chalfant, at the Wylie Agency, and Liping Wang. Love and thanks to Steven Barclay and Kathryn Barcos and all the people at the Steven Barclay Agency.

Thank you to the people who help me so much with my work, especially Doug Foster, Karen Carlson, Tom Weston, Janine Reid and Mark Childress.

Thank you to the people of St. Andrew Presbyterian Church, Marin City, California, especially my beloved prayer partner Elizabeth Talley.